Co-use of Alcohol, Tobacco and Marijuana: Free Yourself from Abuse and Dependence

By

John A. Looney

Table of Contents

Introduction

Cannabis, cigarettes, and alcohol are some of the most widely consumed substances. Depending on the cocktail mix taken, long-term use of these drugs may change normal brain circuitry in a variety of ways. Additionally, it has been shown that co-using cigarettes and alcohol reduces the amount of gray matter.

According to research, consuming marijuana and alcohol may act as "gateways" to taking more dangerous substances.
Nicotine is another gateway substance that young people need to be aware of. In your late teens and early 20s, smoking or using e-cigarettes alters your brain and body,

which may increase your risk of trying other addictive drugs.

Additionally, vaping can intensify the effects of nicotine, raising the danger.
The use of cigarettes and cannabis poses health concerns in all forms. By deciding not to use, these hazards can only be entirely avoided. Here are some recommendations to reduce your risk if you decide to use tobacco or cannabis:

Avoid combining cannabis with cigarettes, as well as mixing it with alcohol or other narcotics.
To make it easier on your lungs, don't breathe in deeply or hold your breath.
Select different cannabis products, such as edibles. Although they are less damaging to your lungs, keep in mind that they still pose health hazards.
If you are pregnant, suspect you may be pregnant or are attempting to become pregnant, avoid using cannabis or

cigarettes. We are unaware of any safe dose or method for smoking cigarettes or cannabis while you are pregnant or nursing. Avoid smoking or vaping tobacco or cannabis around kids or in your house. Vaping and secondhand smoke are dangerous, particularly to young children and women who are nursing or pregnant.

When you use too much cannabis, you run the risk of being poisoned. The signs consist of:
-very rapid heart rate
-experiencing severe nausea or vomiting
-experiencing panic episodes feeling very nervous, perplexed, or paranoid
-seizures

Smoking affects the brain's chemistry, promotes oxidative stress and inflammation, and has many other negative health effects. Alcohol abuse may have comparable results.

Alcohol abuse, drug use, and smoking are all risk factors for poor mental health. Similar to how increased drug abuse, smoking, and addictive behaviors may result from poor mental health.
This implies that we could become caught in a vicious cycle.

For instance, a person who uses cannabis to treat their mental health problems may become more nervous and paranoid over time, and they may even start to experience psychotic symptoms.

Substance abuse and addiction may cause shame, worry about money, and pressure on relationships, along with concern about obtaining the next drink, or hit.

We may regain control of our moods and emotions by giving up drugs and alcohol, as well as smoking and other addictive behaviors.

Smokers, for example, may erroneously think that quitting would have a detrimental impact on their mental health. However, it may lessen depressive and anxious symptoms.

If you use drugs or alcohol improperly, smoke, or both, there are many resources for knowledge and assistance that might be helpful.

Chapter One

Alcohol, Tobacco, and Marijuana
The three most popular substances in the US are alcohol, cigarettes, and cannabis, and co-use is widespread. The use of cigarettes, alcohol, and cannabis have each been linked to different changes in brain anatomy.

In the United States, concurrent use of the two drugs is more than 60–70% more common among cannabis users and more than five times more common among smokers as determined by usage in the previous month.

Additionally, in other nations, tobacco is virtually always combined with smoked cannabis. Despite the widespread use of both cannabis and tobacco, the interactions

between the two substances and negative
health effects get little attention.
Both marijuana and cigarettes have been
linked to individual alterations in the way
that the brain is wired and functions.

Combining the use of alcohol, cannabis, and
cigarettes is frequent. People approach this
in many ways. One method is to use one of
them while the effects of the other are still
being felt. This involves consuming one after
the other quickly -a practice known as
"chasing"- and combining nicotine and
cannabis to consume both at once.

Using alcohol, marijuana, and cigarettes all
at once is another option.
Combining the use of alcohol, cannabis, and
cigarettes may be very harmful to your
health.

The most popular methods for consuming
tobacco and cannabis are smoking and
vaping.

Smoking is the act of breathing in (inhaling) tobacco and cannabis smoke. People puff on cigarettes, make their joints, and blunt, using bongs and hookahs, or use pipes, bowls, water pipes, and tobacco cigarettes coated in cannabis oil.

Inhaling vapor produced by heating dry cannabis, tobacco, or an extract is known as vaping. It does not burn because of the intense heat.

Combining cannabis with cigarettes seems to have negative health effects. Even if we still don't completely comprehend the long-term consequences, we do know:

The most dangerous method of using tobacco and cannabis is smoking. Breathing issues might result from smoking's direct lung damage.

Vaping tobacco and cannabis has various dangers and side effects. Vaping has an immediate impact on your lungs and might harm them. Vaping has been associated with severe respiratory issues.
Some individuals have medical complications and even die away.
The long-term implications of vaping are largely unknown.

Together smoking tobacco and cannabis exposes you to hazardous chemicals and substances from both, which is detrimental to your health. Tar and carbon monoxide, for instance, may lead to cancer.

Nicotine (a component in tobacco) dependency may result from the use of tobacco and cannabis together. You can't quit utilizing it at this point. You have a larger chance of developing cannabis dependency as a result.
This occurs when you continue to use cannabis even though it is damaging your

health and giving you other issues (such as with work or your relationships).

Cannabis and nicotine use may hurt how your brain develops if you are under 25. Your chance of developing dependent on cannabis and cigarettes increases the sooner you start using them. You run the danger of developing major health issues as well.

Using cigarettes and cannabis together may be dangerous for others around.
 They could inhale your smoke (secondhand smoke) or it might linger on their clothing, furniture, or walls.
People may be exposed to chemicals like cyanide and ammonia as a result, increasing their risk of cancer and lung issues.

You run the chance of developing the following conditions if you use cannabis and cigarettes together:

-making dangerous judgments, such as driving while intoxicated (high or drunk),
-engaging in harmful behaviors, including abusing alcohol, and other drugs, or engaging in unsafe sex.

Compared to persons who don't use these two substances together, those who use more cannabis or cigarettes tend to

-have sadness, anxiety, and thinking issues, including difficulties with memory and learning.

-having social troubles, such as difficulties in one's personal and familial connections, as well as financial difficulties

-finding it more difficult to stop using cigarettes since combining cannabis and tobacco might worsen nicotine withdrawal symptoms and lower your desire to stop.

Both marijuana and alcohol are often combined. Both substances similarly affect the body and mind, causing alterations in judgment and time perception as well as tiredness and slower reflexes.

Alcohol and marijuana may interact negatively and intensify each other's effects. People may act in an unconventional or unsafe manner as a result of the combo.

A person's response to marijuana, alcohol, or a mix of the two may differ depending on a variety of circumstances. Understanding the potential consequences of combining these medications is nonetheless useful.

When marijuana and alcohol are combined, a person's judgment may be affected.
On the long-term consequences of drinking alcohol with weed, commonly known as marijuana or cannabis, there is little data available.

However, as more states start to legalize marijuana usage, the corpus of current research is expected to expand and change.

Currently, the following are some possible effects of combining marijuana and alcohol:

Changes in judgment
Both marijuana and alcohol may impair one's judgment. This impact could be enhanced by combining the two medications.
Combining them may result in memory loss, blackouts, and a higher propensity for dangerous conduct.

According to research from a reliable source, folks who combine alcohol and cannabis are more prone to act sensationally than those who merely consume alcohol.

Combining the use of alcohol and marijuana also raises the likelihood of engaging in unprotected sex with a partner and other unfavorable results in the areas of law, education, and relationships.

Dehydration
Because alcohol is a diuretic, it makes individuals generate more pee. This might cause users to become dehydrated over some time because they lose more fluid than they take in. Combining cannabis and alcohol may enhance this effect.

Studies has shown that cannabinoid hyperemesis syndrome, which causes extreme nausea, vomiting, and dehydration, may sometimes be brought on by prolonged marijuana usage.

Any kind of drug abuse, particularly over an extended time, may result in issues with the heart, the immunological system, and the gastrointestinal system.

The use of marijuana, particularly in young children with growing brains, may cause cognitive decline, poor attention and memory, and reduced IQ.

Both alcohol and marijuana usage over an extended period has the potential to alter the structure of the brain, with the combined effects of both substances being more pronounced.
Heavy alcohol drinkers who also use marijuana have worse cognitive functioning than those who simply drink alcohol, according to recent research.

Alcohol and weed both slow down response times and other cognitive processes which is very important for safe driving.
According to experts, during driving simulations, those who coupled marijuana and alcohol regularly showed poor driving ability.
Additionally, the findings indicated that frequent cannabis users made more driving mistakes than non-users of the substance.

People who use alcohol and pot together often consume more of both substances, according to the authors of a 2017 review. Increased use might make it more likely to become dependent on either alcohol, cannabis, or both.

This is corroborated by recent findings, which discovered that those who use alcohol and marijuana concurrently tend to consume more alcohol more often.

As with the usage of any substance, overdose is a possibility. According to the study, those who use alcohol and marijuana together often consume more of both substances. Overdose danger is increased by high consumption rates.

The results may vary depending on how a person utilizes alcohol and marijuana.

After consuming alcohol, smoking marijuana may make its effects worse. The

major psychoactive ingredient in cannabis, tetrahydrocannabinol (THC), is more easily absorbed when alcohol is consumed.
After consuming alcohol, marijuana smokers often feel a higher high.

Some individuals, particularly those who are not used to marijuana usage, may go "green out." Dizziness, sweating, nausea, and vomiting are just a few of the severe and unpleasant symptoms that may result from a green-out.
Anxiety, fear, and paranoia may also be brought on by increased THC absorption.

When marijuana is used before alcohol, the increase in blood alcohol levels may be slowed, which may lessen or postpone the onset of intoxication.
This conclusion, however, is based on previous studies, and this study has been questioned by others.

Cannabis usage may lead individuals to consume more alcohol than normal if it slows the rise in blood alcohol levels. As a result, there may be a greater chance of hazardous conduct and alcohol poisoning.

Cannabis in other forms, such as edibles, may combine with alcohol to carry many of the same dangers as cannabis in smoking form. Foods that include marijuana or its active components, such as THC, are known as edibles.

Because edibles are simple to ingest in excess, there can be added dangers. Depending on the quantity of THC and other cannabinoids they contain, even modest doses of edibles may result in potent highs.

People who drink alcohol may feel more hungry than normal, which might induce them to eat too much food.

People who are eating edibles and drinking alcohol should watch what they eat very closely. However, it is advisable to completely avoid eating anything when using alcohol.

Alcohol and marijuana use may enhance each other's effects. Although using neither is the safest course of action, using one medication alone is safer.

Those who prefer to combine the two should monitor their alcohol and marijuana intake.

Those who are worried about their usage of one substance or both should see a physician or contact their health care provider

Alcohol

Alcohol is the most often used addictive drug in America, and it has significant impacts. Drinking too much, whether on a single occasion or often, may cause major health issues, chronic illnesses, and even death. Abuse of alcohol alters users' behavior, which may lead to mishaps and violent outbursts. Alcohol addiction has serious and pervasive repercussions. While some individuals can recover from this addiction on their own, the majority need support. Programs for substance addiction may help you or a loved one break free from alcohol's hold.

While many people can consume a moderate amount of alcohol without experiencing negative effects, for some people even one drink can set them on the wrong course.

Problem drinking is not solely determined by how much or even how frequently someone drinks. Instead, what matters is how alcoholism affects a person's life. People who drink excessively and experience problems with their work life, family relationships, finances, or emotions may have a drinking problem.

Identifying a drinking issue can be challenging, but experts or healthcare workers can assist. Some effects of alcoholism can be reversed if detected early.

Tobacco
There are many other types of tobacco such as cigarettes, cigars, pipes, snuff, and chewing tobacco.
In this book, smoking is referred to as cigarette smoking, tobacco use is referred to as the use of tobacco in any form, and nicotine is referred to as the psychoactive component of tobacco products.

The majority of smokers do not progress to other substance use disorders, however for certain smokers, tobacco does seem to be a gateway drug.

People who subsequently acquire alcohol or other substance use issues often start with nicotine.

Young people are more likely to use alcohol, cannabis, and illicit substances if they have a history of smoking, especially regular smoking. More than 80% of young people with drug use problems smoke, get addicted to nicotine and keep smoking into adulthood.

Any cigarette user runs the danger of becoming addicted. Avoiding cigarettes is the greatest approach to avoiding addiction.

Addiction risk may be impacted by many things. For instance, smoking and nicotine addiction are more likely to occur in those with a family history of the condition as well as those who grew up in households where tobacco use was common.

Additionally, smokers who begin while they are young are more likely to continue smoking throughout adulthood.
According to one study trusted Source, 80% of smokers started doing so before the age of

18. Early smoking is often associated with increased dependency later in life. The American Society of Addiction Medicine notes that mature smokers and addicts are less likely to stop smoking.

A higher risk of nicotine dependency exists in those who misuse alcohol, drugs, or both, as well as in those who suffer from mental illnesses.

Marijuana

Marijuana, often known as weed, pot, cannabis, and a variety of other names, is a combination of dried plant parts from the cannabis plant, usually flowers or buds but sometimes leaves and stems.

Tetrahydrocannabinol (THC), also known as delta-9-tetrahydrocannabinol, is the main psychoactive substance found in this plant. The exhilaration, or "high," that users of marijuana for recreational purposes desire is produced by THC.

THC travels to the brain when marijuana enters your body via your bloodstream. The substance targets cannabinoid receptors, which are found in specific brain cells. These receptive cells make up a significant portion of the brain regions involved in memory, coordination, sensory perception, and thought.

More than 100 other THC-related substances are also produced by the cannabis plant, which is collectively referred to as cannabinoids.
Commonly referred to as CBD, cannabidiol is a non-intoxicating cannabinoid that is frequently used medically to alleviate the signs and symptoms of numerous illnesses.

Cannabis may be consumed by smoking it out of blunts, joints, pipes, bongs, or edibles like brownies, cookies, or candies. Additionally, marijuana may be smoked or vaped by users.

Marijuana is the most widely used illegal substance in the United States, according to the National Institute on Drug Abuse (NIDA).

Chapter Two

Use, Abuse and Addiction

Alcohol
Alcohol is easily accessible and tolerated across many cultures, unlike cocaine or heroin. It often occupies the center of social interactions and is intimately connected to pleasure and celebration.

For a lot of folks, drinking is a way of life. When drinking is accepted in society, it may be difficult to distinguish between someone who enjoys the occasional drink and someone who has a problem.
Alcoholism might be difficult to identify.

Although they are not the same, the words alcohol dependency and alcohol abuse are sometimes used synonymously.
Understanding the distinction between alcohol abuse and alcohol dependence is

crucial since they may have different effects
and need different treatments.

You are not alone if you or a loved one are
struggling with alcoholism.
According to studies, more than 85% of
adults over the age of 18 have drunk alcohol
at some point in their lives.
More concerning is the prevalence of binge
drinking, which is admitted by more than
25% of the population.
It's more frequent than you would imagine
that what begins as social drinking can soon
turn into a problem.

Millions of individuals have alcohol use
disorder, according to a poll on alcohol use.
This medical condition is characterized by
obsessive drinking and a lack of control over
alcohol use. Each year, hundreds of
thousands of men and women lose their
lives due to alcohol-related causes.

It's critical to get assistance right away if you or a loved one is battling alcoholism.

Alcohol abuse, to put it simply, is drinking too much and too often. The phrase describes a problematic drinking habit in which a person engages in self-destructive alcohol usage.
Uncertain if you or a loved one are alcohol abusers? Think about the following:

Do you pose a physical threat to others or yourself, for example, by drinking and driving?

Are you failing to complete your obligations at home while skipping out on work or school?

Do you turn to alcohol to help you deal with stressful circumstances?

If you answered "yes" to any of the aforementioned questions, it can be an indication of a problematic drinking pattern.

Alcohol abuse and alcohol dependence vary in that alcohol abuse are not necessarily accompanied by a physical reliance on the drug. Alcohol misuse is evident if you use alcohol to escape from reality or numb uncomfortable feelings but do not feel compelled to do so.

Abuse of alcohol is not something that occurs suddenly. Alcoholism progresses via many phases.

In the latter phases, an individual keeps drinking despite negative social, monetary, professional, and legal effects. Dangerous actions like drinking and driving or combining alcohol and prescription drugs occur from time to time. When a user loses their career or ruins their relationships, they often keep drinking.

Drinking alcohol at a rate that is two or
more times the gender-specific threshold for
bingeing is known as high-intensity
drinking.
Individuals who engaged in high-intensity
drinking were 70 times more likely to attend
the emergency department due to
alcohol-related problems than those who
did not.

Several things might make someone more
susceptible to getting an alcohol
consumption problem.
One's risk for AUD will rise with certain
long-term practices like excessive usage or
binge drinking.
A person's risk may also be raised by the
following elements:

-your ancestry.
-drinking habits and family background.
-traumatizing past.
-absence of parental oversight.

-a mental health problem that co-occurs, such as depression or post-traumatic stress disorder.
-age at which experimenting and/or drinking first started.
-accessibility to alcohol
-poverty.

A person is more prone to alcohol abuse and addiction the more risk factors they have. Protective elements help to mitigate these threats, nevertheless. Positive connections, parental support, and local resources are examples of protective factors.

Drinking Excessively and Binge Drinking

Having five or more drinks in two hours for a man and four or more for a woman is considered binge drinking, which is excessive drinking. Most binge drinkers are not considered to be alcohol addicted.
The majority of binge drinkers in the United States are between the ages of 18 and 34,

with one in six persons reporting doing so four or more times each month.

Alcohol poisoning, alcohol overdose, vehicular accidents, aggression, sexually transmitted infections, cancer (including breast, mouth, liver, and colon), memory and learning issues, and many other health issues and negative impacts that may result from binge drinking.

Alcohol and Pregnant Women
There is no known safe threshold for alcohol consumption during pregnancy, and drinking alcohol may pose several risks. Alcohol is hazardous in all forms.

Consuming alcohol while pregnant is risky because the alcohol is transferred to the unborn child and can result in miscarriage, stillbirth, and a host of physical, behavioral, and intellectual developmental problems, such as being underweight, hyperactive behavior, memory loss, learning disabilities, poor judgment, and vision or hearing issues.

Teen Drinking
Due to peer pressure and the accessibility of alcohol, many youngsters abuse it. 16.1% (or 6.0 million) of people between the ages of 12 and 20 in 2020 reported using alcohol in the previous month.
There were 9.2 percent (3.4 million individuals) and 1.8 percent (669,000 people) of minors who engaged in binge drinking and heavy drinking, respectively.

Teenagers who abuse alcohol may show symptoms including poor energy, possession of alcohol-related items, coordination challenges, mood swings, changes in friends' social groups, declines in academic achievement, behavioral problems/rebelliousness, and the odor of alcohol.

Alcohol consumption by teenagers puts them at higher risk in a variety of ways. Those who drink may be more sexually active and engage in unprotected sex than teenagers who don't. Additionally, these teenagers have a higher chance of being raped or assaulted.

Additionally, they may suffer harm or lose their lives in drunk driving accidents. Alcohol abuse may have negative impacts on a teen's brain in addition to changing how they behave. According to studies, the brain continues to grow beyond adolescence.

Abuse of alcohol throughout the brain's early years may have a harmful influence on how the brain develops, as well as cause learning difficulties and raise the likelihood of later having an alcohol use disorder.

The inability to stop consuming alcohol is, in essence, alcohol dependency.

Asking yourself the following questions can help you determine if you or a friend or family member have developed alcohol dependence.

Do you feel that you need to consume increasing amounts of alcohol to get the same results? (tolerance)

In the absence of alcohol, do you suffer unpleasant emotions and physical symptoms? (withdrawal)

One of the defining characteristics of alcohol dependency is tolerance, as well as withdrawal.

People who are addicted to alcohol often try to cut down or stop drinking multiple times without success. However, since they lack self-control, they usually drink more and for longer periods than they expected.

When a person is dependent on alcohol, there is a physical urge to drink regardless of the consequences, which is the major distinction between alcohol abuse and alcohol dependence.

Contrarily, alcohol abuse refers to binge drinking that occurs even when there is no physical urge. Although alcohol misuse may develop into dependency or addiction, this is not always the case.

List of Signs of Alcohol Addiction

Alcohol interferes with obligations at home and work.

Drinking encourages risky conduct, such as impaired driving and dangerous sexual interactions.

Despite relationship issues, drinking has persisted

Being so desperate for booze that you have no other thoughts

The individual often sips more or for longer than planned

The individual spends a lot of time drinking or experiencing alcohol-related sickness.

The individual throws aside past interests and pastimes in favor of drinking

The regular amount of beverages has a diminished impact, and more drinks are required to get the intended result.

When the effects of alcohol wear off, there are withdrawal symptoms including nausea, a racing heart, sweating, trembling, and difficulty falling asleep.

Despite attempting to reduce or stop drinking, the individual cannot do so.

Even after experiencing blackouts or other alcohol-related health issues, the individual keeps drinking

It is time to get treatment if you or a loved one exhibits one or more of these symptoms.

Smoking Abuse
The tobacco plant contains nicotine, a substance that is very addictive. The addiction is both physical and mental, meaning that frequent users develop cravings for the substance as well as a conscious desire for nicotine's benefits.

People develop a dependence on the behaviors associated with tobacco use.

They also become used to smoking at certain times, including just after meals or during stressful times.

The main way that people take in nicotine is via smoking cigarettes. Pipes and cigars are two other tobacco smoking methods. Smokeless tobacco is retained in the mouth or breathed via the nose as a powder.

Smoking tobacco is risky. Approximately 435,000 fatalities per year in the United States are attributed to smoking-related disorders, according to a study.
This equates to around 1 in 5 fatalities in the US. No matter how long you have smoked, quitting may be very beneficial to your health.

Both the body and the intellect experience pleasure from nicotine. The feel-good chemical dopamine is one of the neurotransmitters your brain produces

when you smoke. This produces a fleeting
sense of pleasure and happiness.

But in addition to nicotine, tobacco products
like cigarettes and smokeless tobacco also
include several carcinogens and other
dangerous substances.
The almost 4,000 compounds present in
tobacco have negative effects on the body,
brain, and mind. Smoking has serious
negative effects on one's health, including:

-lung disease
-emphysema
-cancers, particularly those of the
-respiratory system
-bronchitis
-leukemia
-heart condition
-stroke
-diabetes
-cataracts and macular degeneration are
examples of eye conditions
-infertility\impotence

-obstetrical issues and miscarriage
-compromised immune system
-respiratory infections and colds
-loss of taste and/or smell
-gum illness and dental problems
-the onset of peptic ulcer disease with early
aging
-osteoporosis

People who live near smokers are also at an
increased risk for heart disease and lung
cancer.
Children who grow up around secondhand
smoke are more prone to develop the
following conditions, according to the
Centers for Disease Control and Prevention :

-newborn sudden death syndrome
-respiratory infections and asthma
-otitis media and associated ailments
-addiction to nicotine causes

Nicotine addiction is brought on by smoking cigarettes or using other tobacco products. Because of how highly addictive nicotine is, even occasional usage may result in dependency.

The use of nicotine patches, gum, or lozenges as a smoking cessation aid has the potential to lead to nicotine addiction. However, there is little danger. This is because these products' nicotine content is lower and released more gradually than nicotine found in tobacco.

In the past, it was thought that smoking was only a poor habit and not an addiction since nicotine does not make you drunk or impaired. Today, nicotine is understood to be the highly addictive substance present in tobacco products.

Nicotine levels in the brain decrease after a smoker quits. The mechanisms that lead to the cycle of desires and impulses that sustains addiction are set off by this alteration.

Continuous nicotine exposure causes long-term changes in the brain that lead to nicotine dependence.

Attempts to stop cause withdrawal symptoms that are alleviated by starting up again with tobacco.

Nicotine dependency may manifest physically as:

The first cigarette of the day is ranked as being the most essential by the want to smoke within 30 minutes of waking up, placing frequent smoking sessions throughout the day as secondary.

Smoking makes you feel happy and alert, but those who are addicted to nicotine get resistant to those emotions. Even though they may no longer like smoking, they nevertheless do so because they have cravings and wish to prevent going through nicotine withdrawal.

Nicotine withdrawal symptoms and signs include irritability, agitation, worry, sleeplessness, trouble focusing, and exhaustion.

The majority of the time, these symptoms go away after a few weeks, but for some individuals, weeks or months after quitting, they may still struggle to focus or have intense cravings for nicotine.

There are psychological variables that contribute to nicotine dependency in addition to physical ones.
People acquire "triggers," or conditioned cues, for smoking. For instance, some individuals constantly smoke after eating or during times of stress. These catalysts result in behavior patterns that might be hard to alter.

Anyone who smokes or consumes tobacco in any other way runs the danger of becoming addicted to nicotine.

Who is more likely to smoke cigarettes and get addicted to nicotine is influenced by several variables, including:

Genetics: How the brain's receptors react to the high quantities of nicotine that tobacco products give may depend on a person's ancestry.

Family and friends: Children who have smoking parents are more likely to start smoking themselves in the future. Children who have smoking-related pals are more prone to attempt cigarettes.

Age: The likelihood that a person will continue to smoke and get addicted to nicotine as an adult increases the younger they are when they start smoking tobacco.

Co-occurring mental health issues: Smoking is far more common among those who suffer from mental health issues including schizophrenia, depression, or anxiety.

Other substance usages: Tobacco use is substantially more prevalent among those who use alcohol, cannabis, and illicit substances.

Marijuana Abuse

Marijuana causes several physical and mental side effects. Based on heredity, symptoms might differ from person to person. The potency of marijuana and your method of consumption are other variables that can be at play. Your response to marijuana may also depend on your prior marijuana use.

While many symptoms might linger longer, others are transient. Long-lasting symptoms may cause both physical and mental problems.

Both occasional and long-term marijuana users might experience the signs and symptoms of abuse. Temporary signs that are typical include:

-increased awareness and feelings
-exhilaration and a raised heart rate
-increased hunger,
-altered mood
-lower coordination
-a lower level of attention
-lessened capacity for problem-solving
-memory issues
-difficulty sleeping

Marijuana abuse might result in longer-lasting and more severe problems. Physical issues that last a long time include:

-difficulties with the heart and lungs
-immune system issues
-learning issues

-the following long-term mental complications: paranoia\hallucinations, depression, anxiety, and suicidal thoughts may exacerbate schizophrenia, which already exists.

Abusing marijuana may result in addiction just as using other illegal substances does. Approximately one out of every eleven marijuana users will develop an addiction, according to the U.S. Department of Health and Human Services.

The distinction between abuse and addiction is less determined by how often a person partakes in an activity and more determined by how challenging it is for a person to function without the activity or cease it for any time.
It is hard to quantify the extent to which marijuana consumption leads to dependency. It probably differs from person to person.

You could also develop a dependence on marijuana without developing an addiction. Addiction and dependence both take place in various parts of the brain. But it's typical for dependency and addiction to grow side by side.

The strength of marijuana has grown during the last 20 years. Addiction risk rises with higher THC concentrations.
Addiction is likely to be both physical and psychological, according to the Office of Alcohol and Drug Education. When physically dependent on a substance, your body needs it. When you are mentally dependent, you actively seek out the drug's effects.

The signs of marijuana addiction are comparable to those of other substance addictions.

Common signs include:
-increasing tolerance and continuing usage even if it causes problems in other aspects of life,
-withdrawal from family and friends

Generally speaking, withdrawal symptoms begin three weeks or so after the last usage. The following are possible marijuana addiction withdrawal signs:

nausea\tremors\anxiety
Insomnia, irritation, depression, restlessness, cravings, weight loss

The 2018 National Survey on Drug Use and Health found that as of 2018, 43.5 million Americans aged 12 or older had smoked marijuana in the previous year. The report also found that every day, almost 3,700 teenagers take marijuana for the first time.

Contrary to popular belief, marijuana usage may be addictive and reinforcing. It can also proceed to obsessive levels, which can have a profoundly detrimental effect on a person's life.

According to a 2018 Pew Research poll, 62% of Americans think marijuana should be legalized.
 The U.S. Drug Enforcement Agency (DEA) still classifies marijuana as a Schedule 1 narcotic, making it illegal at the federal level even if numerous states have legalized its usage.

Due to changes in breathing and heart rate, marijuana intoxication might increase the risk of major health consequences for persons who already have physical illnesses like asthma or cardiac diseases.

Addiction may be defined as a brain disorder that manifests as uncontrolled drug use in the face of negative consequences.

Marijuana is a substance, and it may lead to addiction. A report from 2018 indicated that marijuana use disorder among adults between the ages of 18 and 25 had significantly increased.

Even while the incidence of addiction is lower than that of other substances like heroin, alcohol, or amphetamines, it nevertheless affects a statistically significant fraction of marijuana users.

Symptoms of Marijuana Addiction
Marijuana addiction may manifest itself in a variety of subtle ways that can affect every part of a person's life.
The following as signs of abuse, of which at least two must appear within a calendar year:

-Consuming the medicine longer or in higher doses than intended.

-The inability or continuous desire to regulate usage
-Spend a lot of effort attempting to get, use, or abstain from marijuana.
-A desire for marijuana
-Key responsibilities at work, school, or home not being completed as a result of usage.
-Usage yet continuing to have marijuana-related social or romantic difficulties.
-Abandoning social, professional, or recreational pursuits due to usage.
-Continuing to consume marijuana under circumstances when doing so might be harmful to one's health.
-Using despite being aware that doing so may make a health or psychological issue worse or may have triggered it in the first place.

Chapter Three

Alcohol, Tobacco, and Marijuana Use Consequences

The likelihood of concurrent use of one of the two remaining drugs rose when one of them was previously used together with alcohol, marijuana, or cigarettes.

The probabilities of using marijuana and alcohol three times on the same day were often additively affected by the co-usage of alcohol and cigarettes, respectively.

On the other hand, co-use of alcohol and marijuana had little additive effects on the chance of smoking.

The found additive correlations between drug co-use leading to tri-use were greater in women than in men, and sex attenuated some of the observed patterns of co- and tri-use: the association between alcohol or cigarette usage predicting marijuana co-use was stronger in males.

In states that have recently legalized marijuana use, there have been early signs of increases in impaired driving due to simultaneous co-use, which is growing in younger populations.

Epidemiological studies have shown that concurrent marijuana and cigarette use is quite common and harmful, similar to the results with alcohol. According to recent research, up to 53% of current tobacco users also use marijuana, and more than two-thirds of current marijuana users also use tobacco.

Co-usage of these drugs is on the rise, especially among those who formerly used cigarettes exclusively or who reside in places where marijuana use is legal. Additionally, there is data showing that using marijuana or tobacco enhances the chance of using other drugs in the future.

When marijuana and tobacco are used together, as opposed to when either drug is used alone, there is a higher chance of CUD (cannabis use disorder), more psychosocial and mental health issues, a more serious nicotine dependency, greater alcohol intake, and less successful treatment for both substances.

Similar to how co-using alcohol and drugs are frequent among kids and adults, using marijuana and cigarettes simultaneously is linked to more serious drug use and poorer health consequences than using them separately.

For instance, those who use nicotine and marijuana concurrently have a higher risk of abusing both substances to dangerous levels, becoming dependent on both, and having trouble quitting.

Individual marijuana, alcohol, or tobacco usage strongly raises the risk of using a second drug and taking a second drug often had additive effects on the likelihood of using a third.

The two legal drugs that are most often misused are nicotine and alcohol. In adolescents and adults, substantial use of one drug often precedes or predicts heavy use of the other substance.
Even by themselves, smoking and binge drinking poses serious health risks. However, combining the two may have negative synergistic consequences, especially when it comes to occurrences of certain malignancies (e.g., esophagus).

Despite the well-known negative effects of smoking, nicotine itself may have beneficial or even therapeutic effects. Similarly to this, moderate or low dosages of alcohol may have positive health consequences.

There is a lot of curiosity about how these medications function as a result of these conflicting results.

The harmful consequences of consuming cigarettes and alcohol are two of the major risks to global health.
Over the last several decades, it has been abundantly evident that extensive use of cigarettes and/or alcohol has detrimental effects on one's health, including the onset of heart and cerebrovascular disorders, gastric ulcers, and numerous malignancies, including those of the head, neck, esophagus, and even liver.

The widespread legal and plentiful availability of alcohol and tobacco products, as well as other circumstances that may contribute to consumers' abusive and addicted usage, are probable contributing factors to the excessive use of these substances.

In recent years, it has become clear that alcohol and nicotine addiction may be partly ascribed to genetics, rewarding environments, and perhaps even the analgesic properties of the substances.

The two primary causes of mortality in this age range, traffic accidents, and suicide, are both associated with substance use as a key contributor to health and social suffering among teenagers (13–19 years). In addition to immediate hazards, early drug use is a precursor to long-term health and social challenges, such as addiction disorders, mental health issues, and financial difficulties in adulthood.

Because of the fast brain growth that occurs throughout adolescence, young individuals are especially susceptible to the dangers of drug use.

Damage Caused by Drugs Addiction

Even though many teenagers experiment with drugs like alcohol, nicotine, and cannabis for recreational purposes without displaying any overt negative consequences, the data about substance-related damage is convincing.

It is believed that at least half of long-term smokers of tobacco die from its high level of addiction. The majority of young people do not plan to smoke cigarettes for a long time, yet many underestimate how addictive nicotine is.

Similar to smoking, persons who try nicotine vaping may unintentionally develop an addiction to behavior that, although less dangerous than smoking, is nevertheless bad for their health.

There is no safe level of alcohol consumption to prevent an elevated risk of breast, colorectal, and other cancers.

Public health concerns for teenagers include the immediate dangers of alcohol intoxication such as linked violence, sexual assault, injury, and traffic accidents as well as the formation of drinking habits that might have long-term negative effects.

Additionally, cannabis intoxication is linked to a higher risk of traffic accidents and injuries, drug-induced psychosis, and other short- and long-term health and social issues.

Evidence suggests that the detrimental effects of drug use are particularly prominent among young users (under 16 years old) and users of several substances.

Both individual and combined usage of alcohol and cigarettes may have serious negative effects on health. Alcohol is linked to chronic liver disease, malignancies, cardiovascular disease, acute alcohol poisoning (i.e., alcohol toxicity), and fetal alcohol syndrome in addition to its role in traumatic mortality and injury (such as via vehicle accidents).

Lung disease, cancer, and cardiovascular disease are all linked to smoking. An increasing amount of research also indicates that the combination of these drugs may be particularly hazardous; alcohol and cigarettes greatly enhance the risk of some malignancies.

Drinkers and smokers are more likely to get some cancers, especially those of the mouth and throat.
In males, alcohol, and cigarette use account for around 80% of instances of mouth and throat cancer, compared to about 65% of cases in women.
The risk of mouth and throat cancer rises significantly for those who smoke and drink; in fact, the combined risk is larger than or equivalent to the risk associated with

alcohol multiplied by the risk associated with tobacco use.

Co-usage of alcohol and cigarettes seems to significantly raise the risk of at least one kind of esophageal cancer.

The prevalence of liver cancer has sharply grown in the US during the last ten years. More study is required to fully understand the potential synergistic effects that alcohol and cigarettes may have on the chance of developing liver cancer.

According to the American Heart Association, more than 34% of Americans are thought to be suffering from a cardiovascular ailment. Both alcohol use and tobacco use are significant risk factors for many types of cardiovascular disease. There isn't any proof, however, that smoking and drinking together increase risk beyond the sum of each behavior's impacts.

Identifying the risk factors for cardiovascular disease is challenging due to the complexity of the problems at hand.

First off, several different disorders fall under the umbrella of cardiovascular disease, including heart attack, stroke, and hardening or narrowing of the arteries. Second, alcohol's impact on cardiovascular disease depends on a variety of factors, including gender, age, and drinking habits, whereas tobacco has been shown to increase the risk for cardiovascular disease in a dose-dependent manner—the more a person smokes, the greater their risk of developing cardiovascular disease increases.

Overall, moderate alcohol use tends to lower the risk for many types of cardiovascular disease, but heavy alcohol consumption often has negative effects.

The two drugs that are most often abused globally are alcohol and marijuana. They are often used in tandem as well.

There are several risks that you may not be aware of if you are drinking alcohol and smoking marijuana at the same time.

Alcohol and marijuana both have depressive effects. Their effects reduce, impede, and decrease the brain's normal capacity to operate. The effects of each drug are amplified when alcohol and marijuana are combined. A person could as a consequence of this lose control over their activities and perhaps overdose.

THC, the main component in cannabis, might have stronger effects if alcohol is consumed beforehand.

THC, the main element in cannabis, and ethanol, the active ingredient in alcohol, both influence our:

-Having restraint
-Making choices
-Judgment
-Reflexes\Movement
-Time perception
-Emotions
-Inhibitions
-Senses
-Sexual inclination and behavior

Both marijuana and alcohol may impair our senses of sight, hearing, smell, touch, and taste. Our senses get increasingly warped the more booze and cannabis we ingest.

Both cannabis and alcohol have significant impacts on the prefrontal cortex of the brain, which is in charge of processing sensory information. This might result in our minds creating ideas based on incorrect information we get from our environment, which is never a good thing!

Cannabis comes in a variety of forms and THC concentrations. The effects of the substance are more evident the greater the THC level. Alcohol with a greater ethanol concentration has the same effects.

A habitual marijuana and alcohol user will be less susceptible to the combined effects of the two substances than a casual or new user. However, combining the two medications typically has a unique set of risks and hazards.

Long-term risks of using alcohol when using marijuana include:

-impaired cognitive abilities and distorted sense of time
-impaired fine motor abilities and movement
-impairment poor judgment

-sluggish reflexes
-sluggish breathing faster heart rate
-inability to decide critical matters
-diminished inhibitions
-a lack of cooperation
-vision distortion
-impairment of short-term memory when under the influence
-increased risk of injuries and accidents
-Increased chance of contracting sexually transmitted illnesses, infections, and unintended pregnancies.
-increased risk of being physically or sexually abused.
-increased sexual desire paired with lowered boundaries, bad judgment, and poor decision-making may result in undesirable sexual decisions and outcomes.
-increased chance of having hallucinations (audio or visual)
-increased chances of paranoia, overdose, and respiratory depression

-increased chance of suffering a negative outcome (anxiety, hallucinations, nausea, vomiting, and paranoia)

The following are some long-term risks of combining marijuana and alcohol:

Cannabis and alcohol tolerance is the need for increasing doses of each drug.

Alcohol and cannabis dependence, which may lead to withdrawal symptoms if not enough of either substance is ingested

Both cannabis and alcohol addiction is incurable, life-threatening brain diseases. excessive alcohol intake harms the brain and other organs

Anxiety, sadness, and psychosis are among the most severe mental health conditions. brain damage brought on by high THC and alcohol use.

The liver is among the organs that are damaged when alcohol is consumed in excess.

Regularly combining cannabis and alcohol over an extended length of time may cause physical and mental harm that cannot be repaired by quitting either drug alone or both.

When used excessively, both alcohol and marijuana are known to have a detrimental effect on mental health. What is secure for one individual could cause another to develop a chronic mental disease.

Your particular response to a drug is influenced by a variety of elements, including biological, environmental, social, and biological aspects.

Teenagers, those with a history of mental illness, and anyone with a family history of addiction or mental illness are more likely to experience the negative effects of both of these drugs.

The risk of getting a severe mental health disorder is enhanced when cannabis and alcohol are combined often.
It is typical for someone who consumes alcohol, smokes marijuana, and has mental health issues to not blame the drugs for their symptoms.
To self-medicate, they are probably going to consume more alcohol and marijuana, thereby making their symptoms worse.

The majority of mental health conditions go better when marijuana and alcohol are stopped, but for a small percentage of people, mental health problems will last the remainder of their lives.

Any remaining mental health issues must be thoroughly and effectively handled while addressing a drug addiction problem. If they are not, there is a very significant chance that the person will start abusing drugs again.

Both addictions must be addressed concurrently and thoroughly for the treatment of the addiction to combining alcohol and cannabis to be effective.

In cases of alcohol dependency, quitting alcohol might not only be risky but even fatal. Unless psychosis is present, quitting marijuana or cannabis when there is a reliance is not life-threatening. This does not imply that it is not difficult. The withdrawal effects of cannabis may be very unpleasant and painful.

Residential therapy is often the best option when there are several addictions present, particularly when there is a dependency on one or more drugs.

Stopping both drugs safely will be the first step in recovering from a cannabis and alcohol addiction. Clinical experts advise a medical detox as the most secure method of doing this.

Consequences

Mental Chemistry
The most intricate organ in the human body is the brain. It may only weigh a little more than three pounds, yet it magically regulates both your thoughts and the bodily functions that keep you alive. Alcohol and drugs disrupt the molecules in your body that maintain your brain functioning properly, which alters how you feel.

When you take drugs for the first time, your brain produces a substance called dopamine that gives you a euphoric feeling and makes you need more of the drug.
Your mind becomes used to more dopamine over time to the point that you can't operate properly without it.

Your personality, memories, and biological functions that you may presently take for granted will all start to alter.

Complications in health
The use of drugs and alcohol has an effect on almost every organ in your body, including your heart and bowels. Injecting substances may cause collapsed veins and infections in your heart valves, and substance misuse can cause irregular heart rhythms and heart attacks.

Several medications may also prevent your bones from developing normally, while others cause extreme muscular cramps and overall weakness. Drug abuse over a long period might ultimately harm your liver and kidneys.

Infections
When you're high on drugs or alcohol, you could forget to use safe sex techniques. The

likelihood of developing an STD rises when unprotected intercourse is engaged.
Sharing injection needles may expose you to viruses including hepatitis C, hepatitis B, and HIV. Sharing pipes and bongs may also transmit common colds, the flu, and mono.

Legal Repercussions
A lifetime of dealing with the legal repercussions of drug and alcohol misuse is possible, in addition to the detrimental long-term impacts on your health.
Before hiring you, many companies demand that you submit to a drug test; many of them continue to do so at random even after you start working for them.
Refusing to stop taking drugs might lead to unemployment, which has further problems.

Driving while intoxicated may result in a suspended driver's license, often for 6 months to 2 years. Additionally, you'll be subject to severe penalties and maybe even a prison sentence.

Financial difficulties
Alcohol and drugs are costly, particularly if you use them often and heavily. Your productivity and achievement at work and in school are both impacted by substance misuse. Learning new skills to further your profession is a better use of the time that might otherwise be spent looking for, using, and recovering from drugs.

Your expenses will also go up due to the legal difficulties associated with drug usage. You can see a rise in the cost of your health and auto insurance, as well as an increase in the cost of arrest warrants, DUIs, and legal representation.

Accidents and Death
You are more likely to suffer bodily harm or be involved in auto accidents if you consume drugs and alcohol. Even worse, your chance of dying by suicide as well as murder has risen.

Since the early 1980s, the number of drug-related fatalities has doubled. Each year, alcohol especially causes 1.8 million fatalities and 5.2 million accidents. According to the World Health Organization, drugs and alcohol are thought to be the cause of one out of every four fatalities.

Cannabis And Alcohol
Combining marijuana with alcohol raises the risk of an overdose since both substances are depressants. Both drugs have the potential to produce nausea, vomiting, extreme anxiety, and paranoia. However, since marijuana lessens nausea sensations, it can keep alcohol from being vomited out of your system. As a result, alcohol may stay in your system longer and could harm you.

Your mental and physical health may be impacted by drugs and alcohol.

Drug and alcohol usage has both immediate and long-term bodily impacts.
Several health issues, such as cancer, heart disease, and infections like COVID-19, are linked to alcohol and drug usage.

A substance use disorder (SUD), a mental health disease when drug and alcohol use is continued despite negative effects, affects about 20 million individuals in the United States. When it is severe, substance use disorder is sometimes referred to as "addiction."

Alcohol and other substances may have acute bodily impacts when you consume them. The kind of drug you use, how much you use, and your general health all affect these consequences. Some medicines may have these effects after only one usage.

The use of drugs and alcohol has been linked to several illnesses, including heart disease, cancer, and even stroke.

Examples comprise:

Alcohol and the majority of drugs are associated with heart and blood vessel issues. Heart rhythm problems, heart attacks, strokes, and even death might result from this.

Dental issues: Various substances, such as the dry mouth and tooth rot, may lead to dental issues.

Lung problems: Smoking and drug use may harm your lungs and raise your chance of developing lung conditions including bronchitis or lung cancer.

HIV, hepatitis, as well as heart and skin diseases, are among the ailments that are made more likely by drug injection.

Additionally, using drugs might erode your immune system, leaving you more prone to illnesses like COVID-19.

Harm to the kidneys: Some medicines might cause direct damage to the kidneys or make them work harder than usual.
Alcohol and narcotics may harm your liver, particularly when used together.

Mental health issues: Many medicines have the potential to exacerbate or develop new mental health issues, such as schizophrenia, depression, or anxiety.

Cancer: Numerous cancers have been associated with smoking cigarettes, using marijuana, and drinking alcohol.

Your physical and mental health may be negatively impacted by drug and alcohol use in a variety of ways, depending on some variables. The use of drugs can alter your brain and swiftly cause other health issues.

There are, however, techniques to stop sporadic drug or alcohol use from developing into an addiction.
There are methods to obtain assistance if addiction is a problem for you.

Chapter Four

Treatment and Prevention
Among the leading factors in American mortality that may have been prevented are alcohol, cigarettes, and marijuana. Furthermore, these drugs are often combined.
According to studies, smoking increases one's likelihood of drinking, and drinking increases one's likelihood of smoking. Alcohol and cigarette or marijuana dependence are also associated.

Smokers are three times more likely to be dependent on alcohol than the general population, and those who are dependent on tobacco or marijuana are four times more likely to be addicted to alcohol.

For individuals working in the area of alcohol therapy, the connection between alcohol and tobacco or marijuana has significant ramifications. Many alcoholics smoke, which puts them at a higher risk for repercussions from tobacco use such as various malignancies, lung conditions, and cardiovascular disease.

Studies indicate that smoking-related illnesses claim the lives of alcoholics at a higher rate than alcohol-related issues. The optimal strategy to treat dual concurrent addictions is still up for debate; some programs focus on alcoholism first before addressing cigarette addiction, while others stress quitting both drugs at once. Understanding the interactions between these drugs and their addictions is essential for effective therapy.

It might be difficult to understand how marijuana or tobacco and alcohol interact. It is difficult to distinguish between the individual and combined effects of these medications since co-use is so prevalent and

because both substances affect the same
brain systems.

According to studies, co-use of alcohol,
cigarettes, or marijuana differs by gender,
age, and ethnicity, with males more likely
than women to do so.
AUDs, nicotine dependence, and co-use
seemed to be more common in younger
adults.
American Indians and Alaskan Natives were
more likely to smoke, or to smoke and drink
at the same time, even though Whites were
more likely to consume alcohol. Asians,
Native Hawaiians, and Pacific Islanders had
the lowest rates of smoking, drinking, or
doing both at the same time.

Although there isn't a single or certain
strategy to stop someone from taking drugs
or alcohol, there are things that everyone
can do.

The top five strategies to stop drug usage are as follows:

1. Recognize the progression of drug misuse. Using addictive substances (whether illegal or prescription) for fun is the first sign of substance misuse.

2. Steer clear of peer pressure and temptation. By avoiding friends or relatives that encourage drug use, you may cultivate healthy interactions and friendships. Teenagers and adults both experience peer pressure regularly. Develop a solid manner to say no, come up with a strong justification, or make a strategy in advance to avoid caving into social pressure if you want to remain drug-free.

3. Obtain treatment for mental disorders. Substance misuse and mental disorders often coexist. You should get professional assistance from a qualified therapist or counselor if you are struggling with a mental

ailment like anxiety, depression, or post-traumatic stress disorder. A professional can teach you effective coping mechanisms so you may manage your symptoms without abusing alcohol or drugs.

4. Examine the danger signs. Examine your family's history of addiction and mental illness. Several studies have shown that these conditions tend to run in families, but they may be avoided. Your chances of overcoming your biological, environmental, and physical risk factors increase as you become more aware of them.

5. Live a life that is in harmony. When something is missing or not functioning in their lives, people often resort to drugs and alcohol. You may overcome these life challenges and have a balanced, healthy life by developing your stress management abilities.

Create aspirations and objectives for the future. These will assist you in concentrating on your objectives and in realizing that drugs and alcohol will only stand in your way and prevent you from attaining them.

Addiction is an illness that can be treated, not a moral flaw, so if you are battling with it, know that it is curable.

An urge to use drugs or alcohol results from changes in the brain brought on by substance use disorders (SUDs). Even though it is a persistent mental health issue, sobriety is achievable with the right care and encouragement.

1. Recognize the issue

Recognize that you have an addiction issue. Admitting you have a problem with addiction is the toughest step in recovery. The brain is impacted by substance use disorders, leading it to search for explanations and justifications to continue using.

Having the fortitude to tackle your addiction and its underlying causes is shown by your admission of a problem.

While there are many resources available, whatever treatment strategy you choose must include a strong support network. If you aren't ready to ask for help from friends or family, think about speaking with a therapist, physician, or treatment center.

2. Consider Your Addiction
Spend some time thinking about your values, how addiction has harmed you, and how abstinence will make your life better.

Keeping a daily notebook is the most effective technique for reflection. You may start an addiction recovery plan by keeping a diary to help you recognize trends, triggers, objectives, and motivators.

3. Seek Expert Assistance
Options for residential therapy include:
Individual Counseling
Group Counseling
Family Counseling
Peer counseling groups
Dependence on chemicals Counseling,
detoxification, and drug-assisted therapy
(MAT)

4. Recognize The Advantages of Sobriety
You may reclaim the good qualities of your
life by living soberly.
People in recovery often find themselves
liking these things by intentionally
addressing these aspects:
-a stronger feeling of liberation
-better physical and mental wellbeing
-improved monetary stability
-better communication with friends and
family
-more time to devote to their most
important priorities

An emotional response based on experience is brought on by a trigger. With addiction, a trigger often results in a strong need to relapse.

Among the typical catalysts are:
-Stress
-Unpleasant Feelings
the environment
-Community Isolation
-Physical or Mental Illness

Once we can recognize these triggers, we can control them by learning effective coping mechanisms.

5. Modify Your Setting
The likelihood of relapsing is significantly increased when someone stops using drugs or alcohol but keeps up their old routines or habits. Avoid the people, places, and circumstances that set off your need to use to support your recovery.

During healing, a lot of things may alter,
including:
Your stress management techniques, the
people you spend time with, and your
hobbies

6. Workout
Working up a sweat while improving your
general health and well-being will also cause
endorphins to naturally release.
Exercise is one of the greatest ways to quit
addictions and is often recommended.

Exercise is not only a fantastic diversion but
it may also:
Reestablish normal brain activity
Reduce tension and stress
Enhance sleep
Reduce desires
Boost self-esteem

7. Recognize the past
It is normal to feel guilty or ashamed about
your addiction, previous deeds, or bad
conduct. Making apologies to yourself and
others can help you cope with these feelings
as you advance in your recovery.

Once we have come to terms with the past,
we may give ourselves the chance to change
in the future.

8. Request Help
It needs patience, drive, and encouragement
to recover. It might be difficult, but the
advantages of getting treatment and starting
the journey outweigh the hazards of
continuing to use drugs or alcohol.

Request affection and assistance
The support required for persons battling a
drug misuse problem is provided by family
and friends. Sessions with a family
counselor assist them in learning more
about how to quit drug misuse.

You have the greatest chance of maintaining
a new lifestyle free from alcohol and drugs
when you include the people you love the
most in your recovery.

Your family may, for instance, make sure
that no illegal drugs are stored in your
house.

There are things we can all do to prevent
drug and/or alcohol misuse even if it's
almost impossible to stop everyone from
consuming illegal substances.

You may be able to stop those around you
from using drugs by imparting this
information to them.

9. Handle the pressures of life. People
nowadays feel that they deserve a nice break
or a reward since they are overworked and
overburdened. However, drugs ultimately
simply increase life's stress, and a lot of us
all too often fail to see this in the heat of the
moment. Find other methods to relieve
tension and relax to avoid utilizing drugs as
a reward. Start working out, reading a good

book, helping the less fortunate, or making something. Anything uplifting and soothing may divert attention from the use of drugs as a stress reliever.

10. Investigate each risk factor. You have a better chance of overcoming your biological, environmental, and physical risk factors if you are aware of them. Risk factors for drug misuse include a family history of drug use, living in a drug-friendly environment, and/or having drug-using relatives.

It is crucial to treat both addictions due to the mortality and morbidity linked to alcohol and tobacco usage. Some of the causes of these illnesses' frequent co-occurrence are starting to be explained through research.
Although combining therapy may be the most efficient strategy to treat concurrent addictions, treating co-occurring illnesses remains difficult.

Adolescents and other special populations provide extra difficulties, but research is looking for novel tactics for these groups. Even while there is still more to be done, it is evident that research is already making a difference in the lives of those who have concurrent addictions to alcohol and cigarettes.

Alcohol Addiction Therapy
Alcohol abuse and alcohol dependence are treated in slightly different ways, and there is a distinction between the two.

It's crucial to understand the distinction between alcohol abuse and alcohol dependency before seeking the appropriate form of assistance.

But the first step is always the same: admitting there is a problem and being eager to seek assistance.

Getting assistance is the next step. A variety of professional services and support organizations provide this.

Recognized alcoholism treatment options include the following:

Self-help: Some persons with alcoholism can cut down on their drinking or stop altogether without the assistance of a professional. Self-help books may be bought online, and websites like Trusted Source provide free information.

Counseling: A skilled counselor may assist the individual in sharing their issues and then coming up with a strategy to stop drinking. Alcoholism is often treated with cognitive behavioral therapy (CBT).

Treatment of underlying issues: Self-esteem, stress, anxiety, depression, and other mental health issues may be present. These issues must also be addressed since they may make drinking alcohol more dangerous. Treatment will also be required for common alcohol-related conditions including hypertension, liver illnesses, and even cardiac problems.

Residential programs: These may include specialized professional assistance, individual or group treatment, support groups, education, engagement of the family, exercise therapy, and a variety of ways for treating alcohol abuse. For some individuals, being physically cut off from temptation is beneficial.
Antabuse (disulfiram), a drug, creates a significant response when someone consumes alcohol. This reaction includes nausea, flushing, vomiting, and headaches. It serves as a deterrent, but it won't address the need to drink or permanently fix the issue.

Naltrexone (ReVia), a drug for cravings, may help lessen the impulse to consume alcohol. With cravings, acamprosate (Campral) may be helpful.

Detoxification: Drugs may assist stop withdrawal symptoms (also known as DTs, or delirium tremens) that might happen after stopping. Most treatments last 4 to 7 days. A common benzodiazepine drug used for detoxification is chlordiazepoxide (detox).

Abstinence: Some individuals successfully finish detox, but they soon or later start drinking again. As time passes, having access to therapy, medical assistance, support groups, and family support may all help the person stay away from alcohol.

Alcoholics Anonymous: Alcoholics Anonymous is a worldwide fellowship of people who have had alcohol-related issues. It is accessible practically everywhere, unprofessional, self-sufficient, multicultural, and apolitical. There are no restrictions on age or education. Anyone who wants to quit drinking is welcome to join.

Consider seeking professional treatment if you wish to assist a loved one or friend who struggles with alcoholism in recovering from their addiction.

Addiction Treatment for Smokers
Tobacco addiction is treatable in numerous ways. However, it may be quite challenging to control this addiction. Many users discover that the ritual of smoking may trigger relapse even after their nicotine cravings have subsided.

For people struggling with a tobacco addiction, there are different treatment methods available:

As a kind of nicotine replacement treatment, the patch (NRT). It's a little sticker that you attach to your back or arm that resembles a bandage. Low quantities of nicotine are administered to the body through the patch. This aids in weaning the body off of it gradually.

Tobacco gum
Nicotine gum is an additional NRT that may assist those who need the oral fixation of smoking or chewing. This happens often because individuals who are trying to stop smoking sometimes feel the impulse to eat. Additionally, the gum provides very little nicotine levels to assist you in controlling cravings.

Inhaler or spray
Low dosages of nicotine delivered by nicotine sprays and inhalers without the use of cigarettes may be helpful. These are generally accessible and over the counter. Nicotine enters the lungs after being breathed via the spray.

Medications
Some medical professionals advise using medication to treat tobacco addiction. Some antidepressants or medications for the high blood pressure may be able to help you control your urges. Varenicline is a medicine that is often used (Chantix). Some physicians recommend bupropion (Wellbutrin). Because it may lessen your urge to smoke, this antidepressant is used off-label for smoking cessation.

Behavioral and Psychological therapies
Some tobacco users find success with techniques like:

-hypnotherapy
-psychological counseling
-neuroscience-based linguistics

These techniques assist the user in altering their perception of addiction. They attempt to change the emotions or actions that your brain has associated with smoking.

A variety of approaches must be used to treat tobacco addiction. Remember that what works for one individual may not function for another. You should discuss the kind of therapy you ought to attempt with your doctor.

Marijuana addiction treatment
The U.S. Food and Drug Administration (FDA) has not yet authorized any drugs to aid in the treatment of marijuana use disorder. Instead, behavioral treatments, which are often used to treat other drug use disorders, might be utilized as a part of treatment:

Cognitive-behavioral therapy assists clients in identifying and changing harmful behaviors. This may improve one's capacity for self-control, particularly about drug usage.

The core of contingency management is a rewards-based program, which offers a reward when the desired behavior is shown and removes such benefits otherwise.

The goal of motivational enhancement therapy is to promote rapid improvement that is driven by the patient's desire for change and commitment to therapy.

These behavioral treatments are provided by reputable treatment facilities around the country, often as outpatient and inpatient, or residential, options.

Remember that marijuana is still a strong substance that has the potential to become addictive even if the general public's opinion of marijuana usage continues to lean in that direction.

It's never too late to ask for assistance if you or a loved one is experiencing the debilitating aftereffects of addiction and you don't know where to turn.

Chapter Five

Benefits of Giving Up Alcohol, Tobacco, and Marijuana on Your Health

Learning to stop using alcohol, cigarettes, and marijuana as well as adopting a better lifestyle that includes regular exercise and good nutrition are also important components of rehabilitation. While every person is different, many individuals who stay sober for a long time find that attaining a healthy weight is a feasible objective.

Alcohol, tobacco, or marijuana addiction with a wide range of mental illnesses, including depression, anxiety, bipolar disorder, and schizophrenia, often co-occur.

9.2 million American individuals suffered both mental illness and a drug use problem in 2018, but only about 60% got treatment, according to the National Survey on Drug Use and Health.

While researchers are still trying to pinpoint the precise connection, we do know that many individuals use alcohol and other illegal drugs as a kind of self-medication for the symptoms of mental illness. But they may be unaware that combining alcohol with drugs like nicotine or marijuana eventually makes mental disorders worse. So, when you quit drinking, these symptoms will lessen.

Your mental health will start to improve as you strive toward your sober objectives, both little and large, and become healthier overall.
This might include improved self-esteem and respect for oneself, as well as less anxiety and depressive symptoms.

Advantages of reducing or quitting alcohol

1.Better connections with the people you care about may result from improving your relationship with alcohol.

This might imply:

More time spent together in harmony and fewer fights
The opportunity to connect across various activities
Less stress

2.Absence of hangovers
Hangover is the depressive state that often follows a night of drinking.
It might be a relief to awaken in the morning with a clear brain and plenty of energy. You can use your leisure time more effectively if you do this.

You may have fresh experiences that don't center around the bar by shifting the emphasis away from booze.

3.More cash
Depending on how much you consume, reducing down might result in significant financial savings.
One of the finest things you can do for your health is to stop drinking or reduce down.

Among the immediate advantages of reducing down or taking a break are:

-decreased blood sugar
-blood pressure reduction
-reduced alcohol-related side effects, such as
-headaches, heartburn, indigestion, and upset stomach

Depression, high blood pressure, or skin disorders like rosacea might be improved by decreased fatty buildup around the liver. greater energy and better sleep weight loss vitamins B1 and B12, folic acid, and zinc are better absorbed, and there are fewer injuries.

Long-term advantages come from adhering to the suggested weekly low-risk drinking recommendations.

They include significantly lowering your risk of:

-blood pressure issues and strokes

-both anxiety and depression

-seven types of cancer

-several other alcohol-related problems

-liver disease

4.Loss of weight
Alcohol and pure fat have almost identical calorie counts per gram. Reducing your alcohol consumption may aid in weight loss.

Gaining weight may also result from late-night nibbling after drinking and junk food binges after a night out.

5.Improved sleep
The quantity of rapid eye movement (REM)
sleep you receive might be decreased by
alcohol. Your daytime focus may suffer as a
result of feeling sleepy.

Your body may take some time to become
used to sleeping without alcohol. When you
do, you ought to feel more relaxed and
energized.

Drinking in moderation is not an issue.
However, the likelihood that you may
endanger your health if you drink more than
the advised daily limits increases. Usually,
the negative effects of alcohol don't surface
for many years. And by then, significant
health issues may have arisen.

The multiple negative consequences of
routinely exceeding the advised limits of
alcohol use include liver issues, decreased
fertility, high blood pressure, an increased

risk of different malignancies, heart disease, and neurological damage.

It's not always simple to stop drinking, particularly if you've been abusing alcohol for a while. However, there are several advantages, both mental and physical, to taking the necessary measures to quit drinking. Here, we go through a handful of these advantages to give you more incentive to give up drinking forever.

Heavy Drinking and Health Risks
It's beneficial to grasp the dangers of heavy alcohol usage before learning about the advantages of stopping. Numerous elements of your health might be negatively impacted by heavy drinking, increasing your risk of:

Alcoholic liver disease
Anxiety
Arrhythmia (irregular heartbeat) (irregular heartbeat)

Cancer
Cirrhosis\sDementia
Depression
intestinal problems
Fibrosis
Loss of hearing
High blood pressure
Pancreatitis
HIV/AIDS, a sexually transmitted disease
Stroke

You will start to feel better—possibly better than you have in years—as the alcohol starts to leave your system and you develop healthy habits.

Benefits of Recovery for Health
According to research, after you quit drinking, some of the harm done to your stomach, liver, brain, and cardiovascular system will gradually repair. Your physical and mental health will start to recover after the transient if sometimes severe pain of

alcohol withdrawal symptoms has passed.
Here are several to think about.

Greater Skin Quality
Do you know what "alcoholic face" means?
This expression is used to describe the
damaging consequences that drinking too
much alcohol may have on the skin,
including:

capillaries ruptured on the face and nose
Dehydration results in dry skin.
Jaundice and inflammation (with chronic,
long-term use)
decreased collagen production, resulting in
sagging, loose skin.
The inflammatory skin condition psoriasis
has also been connected to heavy alcohol
drinking. When you quit drinking, your
body eventually gives your skin its natural
suppleness back, and the redness and
yellowing around your eyes gradually go
away.

Better Nutrition
Your body may get depleted of essential nutrients if you drink. Additionally, a lot of persons with alcohol use disorders have a tendency to "drink" their meals rather than consuming the recommended amounts of carbs, protein, fat, vitamins, and minerals for their bodies.

Even the digestion, storage, use, and excretion of nutrients may be affected by alcohol. As a consequence, many heavy drinkers experience malnutrition. Your body may start to absorb healthy nutrients if you quit drinking and start forming healthier habits.

Alcohol's Impact on Nutrition Can Reduce Cancer Risk
A recognized carcinogen is alcohol. The Centers for Disease Control and Prevention (CDC) state that drinking more alcohol increases your chance of getting some cancers, such as:

Mammary cancer
Rectal and colon cancer
stomach cancer
throat cancer
liver tumor
mouth cancer
Mouth cancer
According to the American Society of
Clinical Oncology, restricting alcohol
consumption while receiving cancer therapy
may help prevent harmful side effects.
Recurrence of cancer or the emergence of
secondary primary tumors are examples of
this (SPTs).

Cardiovascular Risk is Lower
Your heart will appreciate you if you stop
drinking. This is because heavy drinkers are
up to six times more likely than light
drinkers to have a cardiovascular incident
within a week and nearly twice as likely to
encounter one within 24 hours.

No of how much alcohol is drunk, a 2021 research encompassing 371,463 adults discovered that alcohol usage raises the risk of cardiovascular disease. However, excessive alcohol usage is particularly linked to a higher risk of cardiac issues. Some of them are:

Heart fibrillation (irregular heart rhythm) enlarged heart disease
chest pain
Studies have also linked drinking alcohol to a higher risk of stroke, particularly in those under the age of 45.

Improved memory and reasoning
The hippocampus, a region of the brain important for memory and learning, may atrophy as a result of heavy drinking.

A year or more of alcohol abstinence may be necessary for anatomical alterations in the brain to partly reverse. Giving up alcohol may also help counteract detrimental effects on cognitive processes, such as those involved in problem-solving, memory, and attention.

It takes far more work to achieve long-term sobriety and lead an alcohol-free lifestyle than to stop drinking altogether. Therefore, praise yourself if you've quit drinking and started down the path to recovery.

These advantages are only getting started. The longer you abstain from alcohol, the greater progress you'll see. This includes improvements in your general health, relationships, work or academic performance, money, and other areas.

As your mind and body recover and you retrain your life to function without alcohol, do your best to be patient. At the same time, be proud of how far you've already gone.

Health Advantages of Giving Up Smoking

No matter your age, no matter how much, and no matter how long you've smoked, giving up offers health advantages.
One of the most significant steps a person can take to enhance their health is to stop smoking. Regardless of their age or length of smoking, this is accurate.

Giving up smoking:
Improves quality of life and improves health. Gives people a chance to live longer and can increase their life expectancy by up to 10 years.

Lowers the chance of a wide range of harmful health impacts, including cancer, poor reproductive results, cardiovascular disease, and chronic obstructive pulmonary disease (COPD).

Helps those who have already been given a COPD or coronary heart disease diagnosis.

Promotes both pregnant women's health and the health of their developing children.

Lessens the financial toll that smoking has on smokers, healthcare systems, and society as a whole.

While there are larger health advantages to stopping earlier in life, quitting smoking is good for your health at any age. Quitting smoking has advantages for everyone, including those who have smoked for a long time or severely.

The best method to avoid exposing friends, family, colleagues, and other people to the health concerns of secondhand smoke is to stop smoking.

Quitting smoking has advantages for those with coronary heart disease as well.
After receiving a coronary heart disease diagnosis, one should stop smoking:

lowers the chance of dying too soon.
decreases the chance of dying from heart disease, having a heart attack for the first time, or having another heart attack.

Smoking Cessation Benefits for Respiratory Health
One of the most crucial steps smokers may take to lower their risk of respiratory problems is to stop smoking.

Quitting smoking lowers the chance of getting COPD.
lowers the loss of lung function over time and delays the advancement of COPD in those with the condition.
lessens respiratory symptom severity (e.g., cough, sputum production, wheezing).

cuts down on respiratory infections (e.g. bronchitis, pneumonia).
may enhance lung function, lessen symptoms, and enhance the effectiveness of asthma medication.

Giving up smoking may improve the outlook and lower the chance of early mortality for cancer survivors.

Quitting smoking reduces the risk of 12 different cancers, including those of the mouth, throat, voice box, esophagus, lung, acute myeloid leukemia (AML), liver, stomach, pancreas, kidney, colon, and cervix.

The benefits of quitting smoking for reproductive health

One of the most crucial steps smokers may take to ensure a safe pregnancy and unborn child is to stop smoking. The ideal time for women to stop smoking is before trying to conceive. However, giving up at any point during pregnancy may be good for both the mother and the fetus.

Smoking cessation may lower the chance of having a small-for-gestational-age baby before or during pregnancy.
minimizes the possibility of having a baby with a low birth weight during pregnancy.
Early on in pregnancy removes smoking's harmful effects on fetal development.
The preterm delivery risk may be decreased before or early in pregnancy.

Smokers who smoke often, such as twenty cigarettes per day, have a much-increased chance of acquiring lung cancer, chronic obstructive pulmonary disease (COPD), and heart disease.

A frequent smoker has a relative risk of lung cancer or COPD that is around 20 times greater than a non-smoker's. Smokers also have a greater relative risk of developing heart disease, which leads to a significant increase in the number of heart disease cases each year that may be directly linked to smoking.

Avoiding smoking also benefits your overall health, which includes how you look. It has been shown that quitting smoking may postpone the onset of wrinkles and reduce the aging process of the face.

The Advantages of Giving Up Marijuana

Marijuana abstinence has several advantages. While some beneficial changes take a few weeks or months to manifest, others happen immediately. Benefits for the body and mind include

increased vigor and drive
a sharper capacity to concentrate
improved memory
better breathing

better cardiovascular and respiratory health
a better, more balanced attitude.
Improvements in relationships, academic or
professional achievement, financial status,
and general health are other advantages.
The treatment of sleep disturbances may
take some time. Many former marijuana
users say that sleep problems might persist
for a few weeks or months after stopping.

The advantages of giving up marijuana are
many.
Whether you're a regular smoker or a
cannabis addict, giving up marijuana can:

1. Make Respiratory Health Improvements
According to the American Lung
Association, tobacco smoke, which is often
linked to breathing difficulties, lung cancer,
chronic bronchitis, and other respiratory
issues, includes some of the same toxins,
irritants, and carcinogens as marijuana
smoke. Additionally, compared to smokers
of cigarettes, marijuana users often hold

their breath and inhale the smoke more deeply, increasing their exposure to tar, which may scar the lungs and cause pulmonary fibrosis, which has a three to five-year survival rate. Additionally, marijuana may open up air sacs in the lungs, increasing the risk of infection and exposure to the germs and fungus often found in cannabis sold on the street.

In addition to helping your respiratory and cardiovascular systems, getting rid of marijuana from your system may offer your body a chance to mend the air sacs in your lungs. You'll also be less vulnerable to pneumonia and lung infections. If you have asthma, you could also see an improvement in your symptoms over the months.

2. Enhances cognitive function and mental clarity
The brain regions in charge of memory, learning, focus, and decision-making are directly impacted by marijuana use. In

summary, consistent marijuana use may cause serious brain fog. Inability to concentrate, memory loss and difficulties learning are some effects of heavy marijuana usage. Although research suggests that certain cognitive deficiencies persist after marijuana use has stopped, other cognitive processes, including memory loss and the capacity to acquire new information, may become better.

According to research from Massachusetts General Hospital, teenagers and young adults who abstained from marijuana usage had higher processing and memory skills than their friends who continued to use the drug. You could discover that you can think clearly and communicate with people much more easily after giving up marijuana.

3. Enhance Your Heart's Health
Cannabis causes the heart to beat more quickly. As THC and other cannabinoids go from the lungs to the cardiovascular system when marijuana is smoked, it may also raise

your chance of having a heart attack or stroke. Chronic marijuana usage may also swell the heart and cause it to become inflamed. The good news is that quitting marijuana reduces heart enlargement, enabling the organ to operate more normally and reducing the risk of stroke, heart attack, and cardiovascular problems.

4. Reduce Your Propensity for Mental Health Problems

Most marijuana users experience depression and anxiety after the brief high of marijuana. A significant portion of marijuana users reports using the substance to reduce stress and flee from their emotional, bodily, and psychological pain.

Regrettably, marijuana may exacerbate mental health conditions. Numerous research has linked marijuana usage to depression. Fortunately, giving up marijuana can quickly enhance your mental well-being. A lot of former marijuana users claim that regaining their desire, energy, purpose, and drive has been just as beneficial as enhancing their health.

5. Aids in reestablishing better relationships with family and friends
Consuming marijuana becomes one of your top priorities as your brain adjusts to it. Additionally, you can start to feel more at ease when high than when you're sober. Sadly, this may start to affect how you interact with your family and friends. Your marijuana addiction may drive you to hang out with other marijuana users rather than spend time with your loved ones.

Additionally, you'll want to keep your drug use a secret from your friends and family to avoid upsetting those who are closest to you and straining your relationships. However, you won't have to worry about those issues once you stop using marijuana. You'll have the time and the motivation to reestablish strong bonds with the people who matter

most to you — your family and friends —
rather than concentrating on acquiring and
consuming more marijuana.
Other advantages of giving up marijuana
smoking for health include

Breathe more easily
The American Lung Association states that
smoking of any sort is bad for your lungs,
and marijuana smoke includes many of the
same toxins, irritants, and carcinogens as
tobacco smoke.
Therefore, if you've used marijuana often,
your lungs could be suffering. People who
stop smoking marijuana may [also]
experience increased cardiovascular
endurance and maybe enhanced VO2 max.
Smoking anything damages the lungs
because of combustion byproducts.

Compared to cigarette users, marijuana
users tend to breathe in more deeply and
retain the smoke in their lungs for longer,
which over time may lead to lung issues.

According to studies reported in the European Respiratory Journal, regular marijuana use is also linked to morning cough, too much phlegm, and bronchitis symptoms in young people.

The good news is that one to three days after stopping marijuana, your lungs may start recovering (and may continue to heal for several years). However, depending on how much and how long you've smoked marijuana, you can sustain irreversible lung damage.

Enhanced memory
Even while the process of brain regeneration begins immediately after you stop using cannabis, it will take a bit longer. Brain receptors that govern neurological functions including pleasure, motivation, memory, learning, cognitive function, and fine motor control start functioning normally again after four weeks of abstinence.

A 2018 research examined the memory function of 88 adolescents and young adults (ages 16 to 25) who used cannabis at least once per week.
It was published in The Journal of Clinical Psychiatry. Researchers discovered that after only one week, individuals who quit smoking marijuana fared somewhat better than they did at the start of the trial. Participants conducted memory tests throughout the length of the study. These results suggest that memory and cognition may be recovered over time and that the negative effects of marijuana on the brain are not permanent.

Improved sleep
Cannabis may aid in your ability to fall asleep, but the sleep you get will be of lower quality. It's typical to continue having sleep issues even after stopping marijuana. In a study published in the journal Drug and Alcohol Review in February 2022, 47% of participants said they had trouble sleeping

after giving up marijuana. Some people may experience insomnia for a few days or weeks after stopping cannabis use, while others may experience nightmares or more vivid dreams that keep them awake.

However, these problems usually go away 10 to 20 days after quitting cold turkey, according to the professionals at American Addiction Centers.

Decreased anxiety
You're not alone if marijuana makes you feel worried, panicked, or paranoid. In a 2013 study, the UNODC discovered that roughly 50% of participants who received THC, the psychoactive component of cannabis, reported having paranoid thoughts. This is due to the amygdala, which regulates emotions like anxiety, panic, paranoia, and fear, being overstimulated by the cannabinoids in THC.

Fortunately, these unpleasant feelings may subside within a few days to two weeks after stopping cannabis. Just be aware that withdrawal symptoms, such as depression, irritability, difficulty sleeping, and abdominal pain, can appear at this time.

Compared to other drugs like heroin, the withdrawal symptoms from heavy marijuana use are mild, but they can still be uncomfortable for the first few days or weeks after quitting, according to a study.

Working with a doctor or addiction specialist to stop smoking is crucial because it can help a patient stop in the right way and lower their risk of relapsing.

Conclusion

Marijuana, cigarettes, and alcohol are probably gateway substances. A gateway drug is any habit-forming substance that facilitates the development of riskier and more severe substance use behaviors, such as the usage of hard narcotics like cocaine or heroin. Young adults who use gateway drugs have changes in their brains that make them more vulnerable to the effects of other drugs and alcohol.

Moreover, since their brains are still developing, young individuals are especially susceptible to gateway substances. Before the age of 25, the brain does not reach complete maturity. Detrimental, long-term effects, such as mental health issues, might thus result from detrimental effects on brain functioning at this stage of development.

If you stop smoking, your skin will look nicer and you'll be healthier. Stop drinking too much, and you'll feel better, remain healthy, and maintain your fitness.

Feel your pulse before you light up the next cigarette. Within a minute, it will begin to rise. Your heart must work harder as a result. Carbon monoxide is carried by blood cells in place of oxygen. Smoking increases the risk of heart disease and many other dangerous medical conditions, such as lung cancer and emphysema.

Drinking more often than the advised daily limits might be harmful to your health. Not only those who overindulge in alcohol or become intoxicated are in danger. The majority of persons who routinely consume more alcohol than is advised are in danger, however, the effects often take time to manifest.
By that time, significant health issues may have arisen, some of which may not be

curable. The risks of developing liver disease, high blood pressure, and different malignancies are among the negative effects. Of course, there is also the possibility of dependency on heavy alcohol consumption.

Alcohol should be avoided by expectant mothers since it may damage the unborn child's development. Alcohol crosses the placenta, and the consequences for the growing baby may be severe.

Lowering your blood pressure or cholesterol, quitting smoking, drinking in moderation, and using the preventative medicine recommended in this book all help lower your chance of having a heart attack or stroke.

Poor sleep and the use of alcohol, cigarettes, or marijuana are closely related. This is because it disrupts the sleep-wake cycle, making it more challenging to go to sleep and remain asleep. Additionally, it relaxes the muscles in your throat, increasing your risk of snoring and sleep apnea.

Alcohol thwarts the immune system's ability to produce enough white blood cells to fight against bacteria and pathogens.
This is why a lot of individuals who drink a lot of alcohol for a long time deal with episodes of pneumonia and TB.

When you stop drinking, you'll also stop getting the many colds, flu viruses, and diseases that you may have previously been unable to prevent owing to persistent drinking.

Following directions during detox enables you to preserve your physical health and prepares you for a productive recovery program.

100% Commitment to Your Treatment Plan

A successful drug rehabilitation program reduces your risk of relapsing. 13% of adults experience problems with both alcohol and drug use.

The best way to stop abusing drugs and overcome an addiction is to do so in a treatment facility or rehab under the care and supervision of medical professionals. You will be able to safely detox once you are in treatment, join a program, and progress through the phases of recovery until you can sustain your sobriety.

It's important to incorporate some of the core principles of the stages of recovery into any initial steps you take toward recovery because they are things you can work on before beginning treatment.

Environmental factors play a role in the issue of concurrent alcohol, tobacco, or marijuana use. Both substances are easily and legally accessible. However, it has also become obvious that biological factors are at least partially to blame over the past 20 years.

According to studies, mixing alcohol and tobacco can increase the high that people get from either substance alone.

The mesolimbic dopamine system, a region of the brain involved in reward, emotion, memory, and cognition, may be affected by both alcohol and cigarettes, according to mounting evidence.
Dopamine is a major brain neurotransmitter implicated in addiction, and brain cells (i.e., neurons) that emit it contain little docking molecules (i.e., receptors) to which nicotine attaches.
The interaction between alcohol and smoke may occur at these nicotinic receptors, according to evidence. People tend to consume less nicotine and alcohol when nicotinic receptors are inhibited.

This same method of action might explain some of the interactions between alcohol and cigarettes, such as the phenomena of cross-tolerance and how users of one substance may develop a need for the other.

Tolerance is a term used to describe a person's loss of sensitivity to a drug's effects. This phenomenon happens when a person has to ingest more of a drug to have the same pleasurable result. This increases the likelihood that he or she may get addicted to alcohol or cigarettes. Cross-tolerance, or the transfer of tolerance from one substance to another, has also been seen in smokers and drinkers.

According to recent research, individuals may be more susceptible to alcohol and tobacco addiction due to shared genetic characteristics. Alcohol and nicotine addiction runs in families. Fraternal twins, like all siblings, share 50% of their DNA, while identical twins, who share 100% of their DNA, are twice as likely to be nicotine and alcohol addicted if the other twin is.

Alcohol and drugs can result in rapid bodily problems after only one usage.
Additionally, substance abuse may result in long-term health issues, incapacity, and even death. Drug and alcohol abusers are at risk for developing health issues.

If you use drugs in high doses or for an extended period, you may be more susceptible to developing health issues.

Addiction occurs when a person uses a drug while knowing that doing so would have negative effects. People who are addicted to drugs or alcohol often have uncontrolled cravings for the substance because addiction alters the brain.

Even while occasional drug or alcohol use does not guarantee addiction, it is a good idea to take precautions if you believe you may be at risk of addiction. This may imply:

Setting boundaries for yourself or restricting your usage

pursuing extracurricular pursuits or activities that don't include using drugs

establishing connections with others who share your aims, whether via Narcotics Anonymous or Alcoholics Anonymous

Utilizing applications for your smartphone or tablet to control your triggers and cravings

Having a discussion with your doctor regarding therapy or drugs

Obtaining treatment for a substance abuse problem

Therapy, medication, and long-term monitoring are the most typical components of addiction treatment. Treatment options include inpatient, outpatient, or a combination of both. Realizing that drug addiction is a chronic illness and that ongoing support is essential is important.

Give your friends and family this advice on avoiding and preventing substance abuse to help promote a healthier, addiction-free lifestyle.
It's time to make a choice: do you want to reclaim your life now that you are aware of the procedures involved in recovering from drug and alcohol abuse?
Take action right away!

www.ingramcontent.com/pod-product-compliance
Lightning Source LLC
Chambersburg PA
CBHW061537120726
48001CB00004B/1603